KANEM-BORNO

THE KINGDOMS OF AFRICA

KANEM-BORNO

1,OOO YEARS OF SPLENDOR

PHILIP KOSLOW

CHELSEA HOUSE PUBLISHERS • New York • Philadelphia

Frontispiece: A terra-cotta head produced by the Sao people of Kanem-Borno, dating from the 12th or 13th century.

On the Cover: An artist's rendering of a terra-cotta head from Woulki in Cameroon; in the background, a landscape along the shores of Lake Chad.

CHELSEA HOUSE PUBLISHERS
Editorial Director Richard Rennert
Executive Managing Editor Karyn Gullen Browne
Copy Chief Robin James
Picture Editor Adrian G. Allen
Art Director Robert Mitchell
Manufacturing Director Gerald Levine
Assistant Art Director Joan Ferrigno

THE KINGDOMS OF AFRICA
Senior Editor Martin Schwabacher

Staff for KANEM-BORNO
Assistant Editor Catherine Iannone
Editorial Assistant Sydra Mallery
Designer Cambraia Magalhães
Picture Researcher Pat Burns
Cover Illustrator Bradford Brown

First Printing
1 3 5 7 9 8 6 4 2

Library of Congress Cataloging-in-Publication Data

Koslow, Philip.
  Kanem-Borno: 1,000 years of splendor / Philip Koslow.
    p. cm.—(The Kingdoms of Africa)
Includes bibliographical references and index.
    ISBN 0-7910-3129-2
            0-7910-2944-1 (pbk.)

1. Kanem-Bornu Empire—History—Juvenile literature. I. Title. II. Series.
DT515.9.B6K67 1995

94-31094
CIP

B+T 10/96 15.95/11.87

CONTENTS

Titles in
THE KINGDOMS OF AFRICA

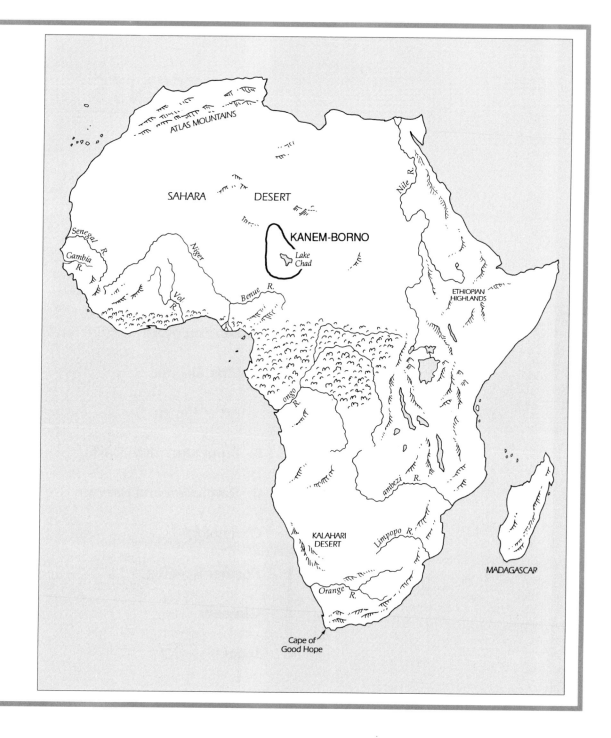

"CIVILIZATION AND MAGNIFICENCE"

On a sunny morning in July 1796, Mungo Park, a Scottish doctor turned explorer, achieved a major goal of his long and difficult trek through West Africa when he reached the banks of the mighty Niger River. Along the river was a cluster of four large towns, which together made up the city of Segu, the principal settlement of the Bambara people. The sight of Segu dazzled Park as much as the spectacle of the broad, shining waterway. "The view of this extensive city," he wrote, "the numerous canoes upon the river; the crowded population; and the cultivated state of the surrounding country, formed altogether a prospect of civilization and magnificence, which I little expected to find in the bosom of Africa."

Park's account of his journey, *Travels in the Interior Districts of Africa*, became a best-seller in England. But his positive reflections on Africa were soon brushed aside by the English and other Europeans, who were engaged in a profitable slave trade along the West African coast and would eventually carve up the entire continent into colonies. Later explorers such as Richard Burton, who spoke of the "childishness" and "backwardness" of Africans, achieved more lasting fame than did Park, who drowned during a second expedition to Africa in 1806. Thus it is not surprising that 100 years after Park's arrival at Segu, a professor at England's Oxford University could write with bland self-assurance that African history before the arrival of Europeans had been nothing more than "blank, uninteresting, brutal barbarism." The professor's opinion was published when the British Empire was at its height, and it represented a point of view that was necessary to justify the exploitation of Africans. If, as the professor claimed, Africans had lived in a state of chaos throughout their history, then their European conquerors could believe that they were doing a noble deed by imposing their will and their way of life upon Africa.

7

A relief map of Africa, indicating the territory once controlled by Kanem-Borno.

Mungo Park (1771–1806), the first European to report accurately on the source and direction of the Niger. Observing without prejudice, Park found much to admire in the African civilizations he encountered.

The colonialist view of African history held sway into the 20th century. But as the century progressed, more enlightened scholars began to take a fresh look at the African past. As archaeologists (scientists who study the physical remains of past societies) explored the sites of former African cities, they found that Africans had enjoyed a high level of civilization hundreds of years before the arrival of Europeans. In many respects, the kingdoms and cities of Africa had been equal to or more advanced than European societies during the same period.

Modern scientists also reject the idea—fostered by Europeans during the time of the slave trade and colonialism—that there is any connection between a people's skin color and their capacity for achievement and self-government. Differences in pigmentation, scientists now recognize, are based solely upon climate and have nothing to do with intellectual ability. When the human species began to develop in the torrid regions of Africa some 7.5 million years ago, humans were all dark skinned because dark pigmentation protected them from the harmful ultraviolet rays of the sun. However, when humans later migrated from Africa to colder climates where there was far less sunlight, heavy pigmentation became a drawback—it prevented the skin from absorbing the amount of sunlight needed to produce vitamin D, which is essential for the growth of bones and teeth. Hence lighter skin began to predominate in Europe, with the peoples of Asia, the Middle East, and North Africa occupying a middle ground between Europeans and dark-skinned Africans. Rather than indicating superiority, therefore, lighter skin can be viewed as a divergence from the original pigmentation of all human beings

As early as 400 B.C., a West African people centered in the village of Nok, in present-day Nigeria, produced small sculptures equal in workmanship and beauty to anything created by the widely acclaimed artists of ancient Greece and Rome. By A.D. 750, the kingdom of ancient Ghana, known as the Land of Gold, was flourishing in West Africa. When Ghana began to decline in the 12th century, power shifted to the empires of Mali, which reached its peak during the 13th and 14th centuries, and Songhay, whose great days spanned the 15th and 16th centuries. Though their power and influence extended throughout West Africa, the great empires of Ghana, Mali, and Songhay were all centered in the region of the Senegal and Niger rivers. (Only Songhay, at the height of its power, extended into the lands east of the Niger.)

A portion of a statue created by the Sao people of Kanem-Borno. The figure is made of terra-cotta, a form of clay that becomes exceptionally durable after being heated in a fire.

Though these three great empires were the dominant powers of their day, they hardly represented the sum total of West African achievement. Providing a home for scores of ethnic groups, each with its own language and religion, West Africa has always been a region of great political and cultural diversity. Among the most remarkable facets of its history is the 1,000-year saga of Kanem-Borno, whose kings enjoyed a reign of prosperity nearly unmatched by any other in the world.

Chapter 1 | THE LAKE PEOPLE

A 19th-century engraving of a scene on Lake Chad. The largest body of water in West Africa, Lake Chad has been a focal point of human settlement for thousands of years.

In all of West Africa, there is only one great body of water—Lake Chad. Situated at the juncture of the present-day nations of Chad, Niger, Nigeria, and Cameroon, Lake Chad is fed mainly by the Shari, Yobe, and Logone rivers. Before its size was reduced by a series of severe droughts that afflicted West Africa during the 1970s and 1980s, Lake Chad measured as much as 10,000 square miles. In the torrid expanses of the West African savanna, where the temperature commonly climbs above 100 degrees Fahrenheit, Lake Chad has historically provided a refuge for a great variety of living creatures. Hippopotamuses, crocodiles, and manatees coexist in Chad's waters, and the lake is visited by a profusion of birds, among them stately cranes, stout pelicans, and brightly colored widg-

eons and teals. In the past, the surrounding countryside also abounded in wildlife, with elephants, giraffes, water buffalo, gazelles, lions, and leopards sharing the landscape with less glamorous creatures such as hyenas, wild boars, and giant snakes.

Not surprisingly, human beings have also been drawn to the shores of Lake Chad—once a vast inland sea—for thousands of years. Archaeologists have found remnants of fishhooks and harpoons made of bone on Lake Chad's shores. These artifacts date from the Neolithic period (also known as the New Stone Age), which began about 10,000 years ago. At this point in history, when humans began to plow the earth and live in permanent agricultural communities, the vast Sahara region was green and fertile. Around 4,000 years ago, the Sahara began to dry out, so many agricultural peoples began to settle around Lake Chad. At the same time, the northern borders of the lake were visited frequently by the nomads (wandering herders) who still made their home in the dry expanse of the Sahara. The most prominent of these nomadic peoples were the Zaghawa, who eventually founded the state of Kanem.

The drying-out of the Sahara imposed a formidable barrier between the coastal and interior regions of Africa. Because North Africa and Egypt border on the Mediterranean Sea, their peoples were able to engage in a profitable trade with other seafaring groups such as the Greeks, Romans, Phoenicians, and Arabs. The remoteness of sub-Saharan Africa caused it to develop more slowly than the areas to the north and east. But trade relations existed between the coast and the interior at least as early as the time of the Roman Empire (beginning in the 4th century B.C.), when North Africans crossed the desert in horse-drawn chariots. One of their objectives was to capture wild animals for the gladiatorial shows of imperial Rome.

With the introduction of the camel in the 4th century A.D., the long and danger-ous trans-Sahara journey became somewhat easier. (The camel's wider hooves and its ability to survive for long periods without water make it a more efficient means of desert transport than the horse.) The Lake Chad region was ideally situated to profit from the increased north-south contact, because the area between Lake Chad and the Fezzan region of North Africa was well supplied with water holes and oases. A major caravan route soon developed along this axis.

As the Lake Chad region became more populous, nomadic groups began to mingle with agricultural peoples known as the Sao. Ancestors of the present-day Kotoko and Kanuri, the Sao had originally migrated to Lake Chad from the east. Interpreting evidence uncovered by French archaeologists, the historian Basil Davidson has written, "With the appearance of the Sao in the neighborhood of Lake Chad, there [was] . . . the beginning of another civilization. For the Sao constructed towns, fashioned rams' heads in pottery, worked in bronze . . . , elevated women to influence in government, and generally elaborated a mode of life that was plainly a new synthesis [combination] of the African east and African west."

13

This striking figure, part human and part animal, was created by a Sao sculptor. The term Sao literally means "people of earlier days." Remains of Sao settlements to the southeast of Lake Chad have been traced back to the 4th century B.C.

A terra-cotta head belonging to a later phase (12th–13th century) of Sao culture in Kanem. The Sao placed statues of important ancestors in their sacred shrines; small heads such as this one were left as tokens of respect by descendants who visited the holy places.

14

As the great Arab historian Ibn Khaldun pointed out during the 14th century, nomadic peoples always prevailed whenever they confronted agricultural groups; the toughness and solidarity gained by the nomads in their rugged desert existence gave them a decided advantage over those used to a more settled way of life. The Zaghawa, black nomads who like the Sao traced their origins to the Middle East, were able to achieve prominence among their neighbors because they were abundantly equipped with horses and iron weapons. They also had a well-developed tradition of kingship, another Eastern trait, which served to unify them.

An organized state called Kanem may have existed before the arrival of the Zaghawa, and as Kanem developed it was almost certainly composed of a number of different ethnic groups. The Sao, for example, retained their own identity for many generations and were never completely subdued. But scholars generally agree that the Zaghawa gave the emerging state its distinctive character and were responsible for its expansion during the 10th century. As Dierk Lange of Germany and Buwara Barkindo of Nigeria have written in volume 3 of the *UNESCO General History of Africa,* "At the end of the tenth century, the kingdom of Zaghawa evidently expanded considerably, and was no longer confined to the region inhabited by kindred peoples speaking Saharan languages: Kanem proper, lying between Lake Chad and the Bahr al-Ghazal [a major river to the east of the lake], was still the center of the kingdom, but other peoples on the periphery had been brought under its sway. It is undeniable that, from that time on, the largest state in the central Sudan contributed greatly to the expansion of the Saharan languages and the cultural assimilation of neighboring peoples."

Thus from its beginning, the state of Kanem was a crossroads of languages and cultures. The emerging kingdom was not only a blend of East and West: because Kanem's power and prosperity were tied to trade with North Africa, northern influences were also making themselves felt on the shores of Lake Chad. Eventually, the driving force of North African culture—the religion of Islam—was to transform the political life of Kanem as well.

Chapter 2 | THE MUSLIM KINGS

Muslim cavalry in battle, depicted by a 14th-century Persian artist. After the death of Muhammad in 632, his followers conquered and converted many peoples throughout the Middle East and North Africa; however, they chose to promote Islam in West Africa by peaceful means.

The religion of Islam arose in the deserts of Arabia, to the east of Africa. The inhabitants of Arabia, who were mainly farmers and wandering herders, had for centuries worshiped a variety of gods and spirits, many of them associated with forces of nature. As they honored these age-old beliefs, however, the Arabians were in close contact with peoples who practiced newer religions, such as Judaism and Christianity. Judaism and Christianity were based upon worship of a single god. Both religions had been founded by powerful figures who had experienced what they believed to be a direct communication from God, revealing a great truth for all humanity.

The prophet who emerged to express a new religious idea in Arabia was named Muhammad. Born in the city of Mecca in A.D. 570, Muhammad spent his youth as a camel driver and then became a tradesman. At the age of 40, he had a vision of a faith based on the worship of a single god, Allah, who demanded strict devotion, regular prayer, and pure habits in return for eternal salvation. Muhammad quickly attracted a group of followers, but he also aroused bitter opposition among the Arabian tribespeople, who felt that he was attacking their traditional beliefs and way of life. In 622, Muhammad's enemies forced him to leave Mecca and resettle in Medina. There he continued to gather converts, who became known as Muslims, and to develop the principles that grew into the religion of Islam. By the time of Muhammad's death in 632, his influence had spread throughout Arabia. His teaching was recorded in the holy book known as the Koran, which has the same importance for Muslims that the Old Testament has for Jews and the New Testament has for Christians.

Muhammad's followers, led by the prophet's father-in-law, Abu Bakr, set out to spread their faith and culture. By 645, Muslim warriors had conquered all of Arabia and much of the Middle East. From there they moved westward into the central part of North Africa. By the end of the 7th century, the Muslims had extended their power to the Atlantic coast of Africa, and shortly afterward they crossed the Strait of Gibraltar to conquer much of present-day Spain and Portugal.

Despite their zeal for conquest, the Muslims were known for their general tolerance in religious matters. They made no attempt to convert Christians and Jews, whom they considered "peoples of the Book," and they converted those they considered "pagans" only when there was a political advantage in doing so. For this reason, the Muslims did not attempt to extend their rule to West Africa; the undertaking would have been too difficult, and they had more to gain from maintaining friendly relations with their trading partners in the Sudan. (The Arabic term for sub-Saharan Africa was *Bilad al-Sudan,* "the land of the black peoples.")

Black Africans who engaged in trade often found it desirable to adopt Islam in order to cement their relationships with North Africans. However, the farmers, fishers, and herders of the countryside continued to follow their traditional religions, which had much in common with the pre-Islamic beliefs of the Arabian tribespeople. Living in a challenging environment and depending for their survival on the fertility of the land and the bounty of the waters, the country people regarded the forces of nature with religious awe. Many of their religious ceremonies were intended to appease the spirits of the sky, earth, and water; they also believed that a number of animals, such as the snake and the ram, were sacred creatures. Though many West Africans honored a supreme being or creator god, the notion of a single deity such as Allah, all powerful yet removed from the earth and its teeming life, was quite foreign to their thinking and way of life.

When Muslim teachers and holy men (known as marabouts) made converts among the Sudanese, they often did so by adapting Islam to the needs of West Africans. For example, they portrayed

Allah as a power that could cause rain to fall in the midst of a drought or bring about some other beneficial event. And although they usually combated groups that worshiped traditional idols, Muslims rarely tried to interfere with the animal sacrifices and other rituals that West Africans employed to appease the spirits of nature. Indeed, the marabouts often wrote verses from the Koran on scraps of paper and gave these to West Africans for use as charms. Usually encased in a bit of animal hide or antelope horn and worn about the neck or ankle, these charms were credited with warding off harm from wild animals, sorcerers, and evil spirits.

Early Sudanese rulers, such as the Zaghawa of Kanem and the Soninke kings of ancient Ghana, tried to steer a middle course on religious issues. They welcomed Muslim traders into their territory, but they did not adopt Islam themselves or encourage its spread in their domains. From the point of view of Sudanese kings, Islam contained some potentially dangerous ideas, such as the equality all of believers before Allah. Traditional African religions, on the other hand, often credited chiefs and kings with superhuman powers. According to the 10th-century Arab writer al-Muhallabi, the Zaghawa followed this practice: "They exalt

A bronze crocodile dating from the second phase of the Sao culture. Animals played an important role in the traditional religions of West African farmers and fishers, who maintained their age-old beliefs despite the spread of Islam in the region.

20

Muhammad arriving in Medina, as depicted in a Persian miniature. Muslims consider that the Islamic era began with Muhammad's hegira (flight) from Mecca to Medina in A.D. 622. Thus, the year 1 on the Muslim calendar corresponds to the year 622 on the Gregorian calendar, which is used throughout Europe and North America.

and worship [their king] instead of God. They imagine that he does not eat, for his food is introduced into his compound secretly, no one knowing whence it is brought. Should one of his subjects happen to meet the camel carrying his provisions, he is killed instantly on the spot."

By the time of King Arku (1023–67), the Zaghawa had extended their territory northward into the Sahara. By doing so, they could carefully regulate the activities of Muslim traders who ventured south to Kanem. But while protecting Kanem's citizens from foreign religious influences, the royal court itself had been influenced by Islam. Upon the death of Arku, a monarch known by the names of Hu and Hawwa became the first Muslim ruler of Kanem. Lange and Barkindo believe that Hawwa may have been a woman; they also conclude that Hawwa was already a Muslim before he or she ascended the throne: "It is very likely that . . . the pro-Muslim faction within the old dynasty put forward the strongest candidate it could find. . . . The very short reigns of Hu or Hawwa (1067–71) and Abd al-Djalil (1071–75) stand in contrast to the long reigns of their predecessors and may be interpreted as a sign of a serious crisis: after a long period of incubation, when the crucial stage was reached in the growing power of Islam, the Muslims first undermined the stability of the old regime and then brought about a drastic political change."

As a result of the Muslims' activity, the Zaghawa lost control of Kanem to a new dynasty known as the Sefuwa, whose long reign (nearly 800 years) began under Mai Hummay in 1075. (*Mai* was the royal title used by the Sefuwa.) By all indications, the Muslim Sefuwa were descended from the light-skinned Berbers of North Africa and were thus of a different racial stock from the Sudanese. Conscious of being outsiders in racial as well as religious terms, Hummay and his successors began (in Lange's phrase) to "de-Berberize" themselves by marrying into local families.

After analyzing a 13th-century Arabic manuscript entitled *Diwan salatan Barnu* (Chronicle of the Sultans of Borno),

Lange concluded that Hummay and the kings who followed him married black African women who belonged to long-established peoples such as the Kay, Tubu, Dabir, and Magumi. These marriages cemented alliances between the Sefuwa and the dominant groups of the region, who were later to merge into a single people known as the Kanuri. The alliances ensured an orderly succession of kings, by which sons followed their fathers onto the throne. By the 13th century, Kanem had thus achieved a new level of stability and was poised to become a major power in the Sudan.

Chapter 3 | THE DUAL KINGDOM

Once the Sefuwa kings solidified their rule in Kanem, they were able to organize the trans-Sahara trade in a highly profitable manner. By extending their sway into the Sahara, the Sefuwa were able to control the natural salt deposits at Bilma, the largest in the region. Access to salt enabled Kanem to carry on a lucrative trade with other regions of West Africa. Though taken for granted in many modern nations, salt has always been a precious commodity in the torrid climate of West Africa, where loss of salt and other minerals through perspiration can quickly lead to exhaustion or serious illness.

When trading with the North Africans, the peoples of the Chad Basin most often provided slaves (mainly prisoners of war), ivory (gathered from elephants' tusks

and the teeth of hippopotamuses), ostrich feathers, and even live animals. From North Africa came horses, glassware, fabric, clothing, and copper, among other goods. In addition to trade, farming, and fishing, many of the Chad peoples prospered from the raising of cattle, sheep, and goats.

The success of all these enterprises depended on the safety of the trade routes and the protection of the countryside against marauders. Throughout the 13th and 14th centuries, the peace and tranquillity of Kanem was maintained by such outstanding rulers as Dunama Dibalami, who reigned from 1210 to 1248. Dunama's power rested upon his highly trained cavalry, which numbered at least 30,000 men on horseback. With these powerful forces at his command,

24

Dunama was able to extend the borders of Kanem far into the Sahara, eventually controlling the entire trade route between Kanem and Fezzan.

In contrast to Dunama's success in the North, it does not appear that he or the other mais of his era were able to control all the peoples of the Chad Basin or even the lake itself. The Tubu, who lived northeast of the lake, maintained their independence even though Dunama waged a long war against them: according to tradition, the war lasted seven years, seven months, and seven days. Arabic sources also indicate that the 13th-century kings of Kanem launched a number of expeditions against groups who occupied the islands of the lake and various points along the shoreline.

Despite his many achievements, Dunama was blamed by later generations for bringing misfortune upon Kanem. His offense was the opening of a talisman known as the *mune*, which apparently contained one or more sacred objects relating to the kingship and dating to the earliest days of Kanem, before the advent of Islam. According to one Arabic manuscript, "When the thing which was in [the mune] escaped, it called forth and provoked every powerful man to ambition and intrigues, in the government and in high charges."

Much of the intrigue in Kanem derived from Dunama's sons Kaday and Bir, who had waged many of their father's military campaigns. Kaday and Bir had been borne by different mothers. West African kings and other influential men typically had a senior wife and one or more additional wives, and this practice often caused friction within the royal family as different wives and their offspring vied for influence. Thus Dunama's sons, as they achieved success in battle, began to form separate groups of loyal followers. As a result, the ruling group of Kanem was split into factions, eventually disrupting the orderly scheme of royal descent. Kaday succeeded his father in 1248, but upon his own death in 1277 he was succeeded not by his own son but by his brother Bir, who reigned until 1296.

During the 14th century, succession to the throne varied, as kings were followed sometimes by their sons and sometimes by their brothers. Because three kings were killed in three years while waging war against the Sao, the question of succession was ever present. Kanem managed to weather the shifting tides of political alliance until the death of Mai Idris ibn Nikale in 1366. At that

(Continued on page 29)

SAO SCULPTURE

During the 12th and 13th centuries, the Sao people of Kanem-Borno adopted the practice of burying their dead in large funeral urns. The Sao also honored the memories of their ancestors by creating statues of them. The sculptures on the following pages were among the hundreds of art objects unearthed in the Lake Chad region by the French archaeologists Jean-Paul and Annie Lebeuf between 1936 and 1952.

A small terra-cotta head, approximately 2½ inches high. Some of the markings on the surface provide information about the sex, age, and profession of the subject; others represent various forces of nature.

This terra-cotta figure is adorned by a large and ornate necklace. In the course of their excavations, the Lebeufs found many specimens of bronze jewelry in addition to sculpture and pottery.

The Sao often created shrines for the statues of their ancestors. In most African religions, death does not mean separation from the earth: the spirits of ancestors are thought to be living presences in the community, and those who honor them expect to be reborn in future generations.

28

A masked dancer in terra-cotta, approximately 9½ inches high. In African religious ceremonies, dancers often donned masks representing animals. Such rituals were intended to transfer the animals' strength and agility to the dancer.

(Continued from page 24)

point, open warfare erupted between the late king's brother Dawud and the king's sons, who opposed Dawud's claim to the throne. A competing group known as the Bulala now took advantage of the unsettled situation and waged war on the Sefuwa. The Bulala proved to be even more formidable than the Sao. They killed Dawud in 1376, and within the next six years, three more Sefuwa kings died in battle against the Bulala. The Bulala onslaught was so fierce that Umar

29

An engraving of fishermen in the Yobe River, one of the principal waterways feeding Lake Chad. The lake and its surrounding rivers yielded a plentiful year-round catch, so that both fresh and dried fish could be readily obtained throughout Kanem-Borno.

A map of the Lake Chad region, showing the territory controlled by the rulers of Kanem-Borno. The original domain of the Sefuwa rulers was Kanem, north of the lake; to escape attacks from neighbors, the Sefuwa moved their capital southward to Borno during the 14th century.

30

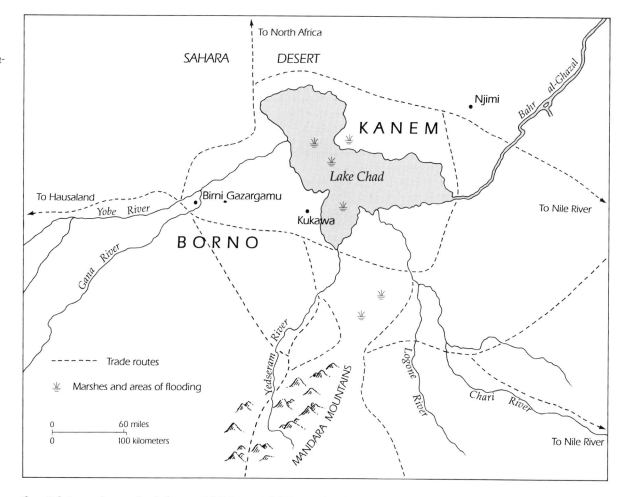

ibn Idris, who ruled from 1382 to 1387, decided to abandon Kanem.

Since the days of Dunama Dibalami, the Sefuwa had been in control of Borno, the region southwest of Lake Chad. In the opinion of Dierk Lange, the Sefuwa had thus presided over a dual kingdom—Kanem-Borno—since the 13th century. Being farther removed from the desert, Borno was greener and more fertile than Kanem, and the Sefuwa were able to step up food production to maintain the growing population of their realm. Borno also provided a refuge in times of crisis.

Feeling incapable of subduing the Bulala, Umar ibn Idris retreated to Borno. Even here, the Sefuwa were not safe from the attacks of their foes. Both Said and Kaday, the Kings who followed Umar ibn Idris, were killed by Bulala warriors. Finally, Bir ibn Idris (1389–1421) was able to repel the Bulala and secure the territory of Borno.

Firmly established in Borno, the Sefuwa resumed their civil wars and power struggles. Stability did not return until the reign of Ali Ghaji, which began in 1465 and ended in 1497. Mai Ali built the city of Birni Gazargamu near the Yobe River, and Birni remained the capital of the Sefuwa empire for the following 300 years. Ali also restored the system of succession by which the mais were followed by their sons, and he curtailed the power of court officials such as the *kayaghamma* (commander of the army), who had often used his position to dictate the outcome of royal power struggles.

Ali Ghaji's achievements were expanded upon by his son Idris Katakarmabe, who ruled from 1497 to 1519. Upon taking the throne, Katakarmabe fought a successful war against the Bulala, swept into Kanem, and reoccupied Njimi, the former Sefuwa capital. Though he now had undisputed control of Kanem, Katakarmabe did not try to reestablish the Sefuwa capital in its former home but chose instead to concentrate on the political situation south of the lake. As Buwara Barkindo has written, "By the early 1500s numerous petty kingdoms had emerged in the Chad basin along the southern border of Borno. . . . Some states were attacked and forced to recognize some form of Sefuwa hegemony [domination]. But more often the Sefuwa tried to enter into some form of peaceful relations with the nascent states. . . . The king's intention must have been to use the emerging states in the building of a regional economic system. Most were encouraged to develop their own economies and to establish regular trade with Borno." As this new economic system developed, Kanem-Borno achieved dominance over the central Sudan.

31

Chapter 4 | IDRIS ALOOMA

The greatest of all the kings of Kanem-Borno was Idris Alooma, who came to power in 1564. The German explorer Heinrich Barth, who visited Borno in 1851 and researched the history of its kings, wrote admiringly of Idris as "an excellent prince, uniting in himself the most opposite qualities: warlike energy, combined with mildness and intelligence; courage, with circumspection and patience; severity, with pious feelings."

Some previous Sefuwa kings had followed Islam merely as a matter of convenience, but like Dunama Dibalami and Ali Ghaji, Idris appears to have been a devout Muslim. He made a pilgrimage to Mecca, the holy city of Islam, in 1571 and promoted Muslim learning at home by bringing scholars and teachers from North Africa and the Middle East. He also tried to increase the authority of the Muslim law courts, which the local people often ignored while submitting their disputes to tribal chiefs. In order to encourage his subjects to use the Islamic courts, Idris is said to have placed some of his own affairs in the hands of Muslim judges, known as qadis.

Idris was responsible for other innovations in the daily life of his realm. Before his reign, the people of Kanem-Borno had followed the original Zaghawa method of construction, fashioning not only their dwellings but also their public buildings out of corn stalks. Typically, the builders would construct an elaborate framework out of the long, tough stalks and then fashion the walls and roof from the thick reeds and grasses that grew abundantly in the Lake Chad

A 19th-century engraving shows a group of horsemen and foot soldiers attacking a fortified village in Borno. The first 12 years of Idris Alooma's reign were devoted to successful military campaigns against neighboring peoples.

33

34

ally plastic [easy to shape], clay and mud also act as good insulators and retainers of heat. Their plasticity allows the artisan-builder wide latitude in working interesting designs and bold relief." Thus the striking mosques of West Africa, with their golden brown earthen walls and dramatic patterns of sunlight and shadow, began to appear in Kanem-Borno.

Idris also strove to improve navigation on the Yobe River, the main waterway near the capital, Birni Gazargamu. Throughout their history, the local people had traveled the river in canoes fashioned from hollowed-out tree trunks. Though sturdy, these canoes were inadequate for large-scale military operations; the process of transporting the king's army across a river could take two or three days. To address this problem, Idris built longer, flat-bottomed boats made of logs from a local tree known as the *fogo;* the logs were lashed together with the rope-like leaf stalks of the doom palm, which grows throughout the region, and the spaces between the logs were caulked with dense palm fibers. To improve land transportation, Idris imported camels from the Sahara to replace the oxen, mules, and donkeys previously used to transport goods.

Above all, Idris was a brilliant and daring military commander who strength-

region. Idris broke with this tradition and began to build mosques out of clay, which was collected from the boggy areas, known as *firki*, that bordered the lake in some places. Richard W. Hull has explained the advantages of this method in his book *African Cities and Towns Before the European Conquest:* "Exception-

ened Kanem-Borno through repeated conquests of neighboring peoples. For 12 years, from 1564 to 1576, Idris rode at the head of his troops, waging successful campaigns in all directions. He went to great pains to modernize his army and paid careful attention to all aspects of military strategy. The discipline and organization of Idris's military machine is clear in the account of a campaign against the city of Damasak written by Ibn Furtuwa, one of the king's aides:

> [Idris] advanced toward them with his army, horse and foot, until he reached their trees and their strongholds. . . . He then drew up the shieldsmen (*ahl al-daraq*) and bucklersmen (*ahl al-majam*) in front of the people in ranks; behind them stood the horsemen dressed in coats of mail (*duru*), with quilted armor (*tajafif*) on their horses, not separated but also in ranks. Then, behind the horsemen, the axe-men lined up so that they might cut down the trees feeling themselves secure from any damage or mischief on the part of the pagans. With them were musicians, those of the fiddles (*mazahir*), those of the tambourines (*dufuf*), those of the trumpet (*buq*), those of the flutes (*mazamir*), and other kinds of entertainment and amusement, so as to strengthen the body in the cutting of the trees, to impart energy and speed, and rid them of the sense of hardship.

With their chain mail and armored horses, the Borno cavalrymen were well protected from the poisoned arrows launched at them by Damasak's defenders. By cutting the trees in the summer, destroying the ripening crops in the fall,

Idris Alooma equipped his cavalrymen and horses with quilted armor and chain mail to protect them against the arrows of enemy archers. The powerful monarch is also credited with recruiting a corps of Turkish musketeers into his army.

35

and raiding the city during the winter, Idris cut off Damasak's food supply and forced the residents to either surrender or flee.

Idris's armies ranged as far north as Aïr in the southern Sahara—where they periodically attacked the fierce Tuareg raiders of the desert and prevented them from plundering caravans traveling toward Lake Chad—and as far south as the rugged, chimney-shaped mountains of Mandara. When he had pacified these areas, he turned the force of his military might upon the Bulala, who had rebounded from previous defeats to harass the Sefuwa once again. Despite the Bulala ancestry of his mother, Mairam (Princess) Amsa, Idris was determined to finally subdue this warlike people. On six separate occasions between 1571 and 1576, he led his armies against his mother's kinfolk.

During the first campaign, waged south of Lake Chad, the Bulala prudently retreated before Idris's forces. Then, when they judged that their pursuers would be exhausted from their long march in the scorching heat of the savanna, the Bulala turned and attacked. According to Ibn Furtuwa, the tactic failed miserably: "When the [Bulala] saw our people come out to fight, and how numerous they were on all sides, their hearts turned and they fled incontinently without pause. Our army pursued, killing and wounding, with swords and spears and whips, till they were tired of it. The enemy's cavalry spurred their horses, and left the infantry behind like a worn-out sandal abandoned and thrown away, and there was no means of safety for those on foot save the providence of God, or recovery from a wound after crouching in darkness."

Having gained the advantage, Idris mounted additional forays into Kanem, driving the Bulala before him. His advance was so relentless that he apparently even struck terror into the heart of the Bulala leader. "Abdul Jalil ibn Bi," wrote Ibn Furtuwa, "had left his wife, the daughter of Yarima, in his house, turning from her when he saw the dust of our armies rising to the skies. For he was certain that the safety of a man himself is better for him than the safety of his wife. So he fled, deserting his wife, since personal necessity is more compelling than the lack of a wife."

By the end of his final campaign against Kanem in 1576, Idris succeeded in bringing all the neighboring peoples under his control. He stabilized the Chad Basin to such an extent that little was

(Continued on page 41)

36

ARTS OF KANEM-BORNO

West African artists and craftspeople worked in a variety of materials, including clay, iron, bronze, and leather. The objects on the following pages all belong to the rich artistic heritage of Kanem-Borno. The first three were created by the Sao people, who ceased to exist as a separate ethnic group after the 16th century, having intermarried with the Kotoko and Kanuri.

A terra-cotta figure of a hippopotamus, approximately 7 inches long, dating from the 10th or 11th century. Sculptures of animals were most likely used in religious ceremonies conducted to ensure the success of hunting and fishing expeditions.

38

A bronze pendant designed to be worn around the neck (the bracket on the left-hand side has been broken off). Pendants protected the wearer against various kinds of misfortune, especially the evils that were believed to arise when religious laws were broken.

This bronze cup, about five inches in diameter, was discovered in a Sao burial place by Jean-Paul and Annie Lebeuf. The cup may have been used to hold the blood of animals sacrificed in honor of the Sao's ancestors.

Part of a harness made of leather, brass, and copper, dating from the 19th century. For much of West African history, the control of a well-trained cavalry was the key to political power.

(Continued from page 36)

written of the ensuing 20 years of his reign, which lasted until 1596. Scholars have determined that in addition to his skills as an administrator and military leader, Idris was called upon to perform as a statesman in international affairs when foreign powers began to threaten Kanem-Borno.

By the 16th century, Africans were no longer alone on their continent. As early as 1453, European sailors from Portugal had landed on the coast of West Africa along the Gulf of Guinea and had begun trade relations that would eventually become a full-scale traffic in slaves, with disastrous results for the Africans. During the reign of Idris, the Portuguese invaded North Africa, only to be annihilated by Moroccan forces at Kasr al-Kabir in 1578. At the same time, a powerful force was rising in the East, as the Ottoman Turks extended their sway over the entire Muslim world and established a formidable presence in North Africa, taking control of the Fezzan oases in 1549.

The presence of the Ottomans disrupted the long-established settlements in the southern Sahara and threatened the security of the trade route between North Africa and Kanem-Borno. For this reason Idris sent six ambassadors to Istanbul, Turkey, the capital of the Ottoman Empire, in 1574. Idris's power was such that Murad III, the Ottoman emperor, agreed to guarantee the security of the trans-Sahara trade routes and to cooperate in controlling both his own forces and the Tuareg. At the same time, Idris came to terms with the powerful Moroccans, who also posed a threat to the peace of the Sudan and indeed conquered the neighboring empire of Songhay during the 1590s. The accords apparently provided for the shipment of arms—including the latest European muskets—to Kanem-Borno.

For all his success, Idris never brought lasting peace to his realm. In 1596, the king was leading an expedition against the Gamergu in the South when an enemy warrior, who was hiding in a tree, hurled a hand-ax at him. The axe struck Idris in the chest and killed him. Thus Idris's great reign came to a sudden and violent end, but he left behind a remarkable legacy. His contemporary, Elizabeth I of England, a shrewd and strong-willed monarch who gave her name to an age and has been repeatedly celebrated in books and films, could hardly have claimed greater achievements in war, administration, or diplomacy. Like Elizabeth, Idris made it possible for his nation to enjoy a true golden age.

41

Chapter 5 | FROM MURZUK TO DARFUR

Throughout the 15th and 16th centuries, Kanem had been confronted by a powerful neighbor—the empire of Songhay. The rulers of Songhay had extended their dominions from the Atlantic coast to the Niger River and had even threatened the borders of Borno, while raiding the Hausa states just to the east. But in 1591, when Moroccan forces routed the armies of Songhay at the Battle of Tondimi, Kanem-Borno reigned supreme in the Sudan, extending its borders as far north as Murzuk in the Sahara and as far east as the hills of Darfur, the gateway to the Nile Valley.

Under the long and prosperous reigns of Idris Alooma's sons Muhammad, Ibrahim, and Omar, Kanem-Borno also achieved the height of its sophisticated culture and political organization. This period marked the emergence of the Kanuri people, who still form the majority of the population in the province of Borno in Nigeria. The Kanuri developed from the gradual intermarriage between the peoples who had earlier migrated from Kanem (principally the Magumi) and the peoples who had been living in Borno when the migrants arrived.

Like the Sefuwa dynasty, the Kanuri effectively blended the cultures of the Sahara with those of the savanna. Their language belonged to the Nilo-Saharan family, distinct from the Chadic languages spoken by all other peoples south of the lake. They also created a wholly individual style in both dress and architecture. Kanuri garments were similar to the burnooses (hooded robes) of the desert tribes but did not simply mimic

43

them. The Kanuri adopted the tobe, a long, loose-fitting cotton garment with wide sleeves. Tobes were either left in their natural white color or dyed a deep indigo. The tobe was usually worn over wide cotton trousers. For additional adornment and protection from the sun, men adopted large white turbans. Kanuri women usually wore wide blouses with more elaborate designs; they took great pains with their hair, sweeping it upward and fashioning braids at the top, creating an effect that resembled the crest of a helmet. The Kanuri became expert weavers and made many of their own garments, though the wealthier members of society favored clothing that was imported from North Africa and Europe.

The architecture of Birni Gazargamu and other cities also reflected a blending of styles. Gone were the traditional round buildings with cone-shaped roofs, made of corn stalks and thatch. In their place were rectangular structures with flat roofs, made of clay. This style of building, influenced by Muslim architecture in North Africa, had also been common in the Niger-based empires of Mali and Songhay. The Kanuri went a step further by developing the art of brick construction, which they employed to build protective walls around mosques and palaces.

Heinrich Barth, who inspected the remains of some of these walls during the 19th century, declared that their workmanship was equal in quality to the finest masonry he had seen in Europe.

In the realm of political organization, the rulers of Kanem-Borno adapted the institution of kingship to create a sophisticated system of government. The mai functioned as the head of state, the official overseer of the land, and the guardian of the Muslim faith. As Buwara Barkindo points out, the mais also retained some of the sacred aspects of pre-Islamic times: "The king was still largely secluded, appearing in public only in a *fanadir* (cage), and people spoke to him only through intermediaries." However, the day-to-day decisions of the government rested in the hands of the *majlis* (council of state), which consisted of the king and at least 12 of the nation's leading officials. Among these dignitaries were the *yarima* (governor of the northern provinces); the *kayaghamma* (commander of the armed forces); the *galadima* (governor of the western provinces); the *kasalma* (governor of the eastern provinces); and the *chiroma* (heir apparent to the throne). Following the tradition begun by the Sao, women also played a major role in the government of

Kanem-Borno. Among the leading female political figures were the *magira* (queen mother), the *gumsu* (the king's principal wife), and the *magram* (the king's highest-ranking sister).

Like many nations of Europe during the Middle Ages, Kanem-Borno was governed on feudal principles. Under the feudal system, all high officials were vassals of the king, and the king placed each official in control of a district or province. (Africans had no concept of land ownership as it is practiced in contemporary Western societies; in Africa, certain individuals simply had the right to the proceeds of the land.) Buwara Barkindo has explained how the feudal system operated in Kanem-Borno:

> All towns, villages and ethnic units were grouped into *chidi* (fiefs) and all major officials of state were *chima*s (fief-holders). These were responsible for the maintenance of order in their fiefs, for the collection of taxes and for the raising of troops for the army. All fief-holders, except the *galadima*, resided in the capital and were represented by their *chima gana* (junior fief-holders). . . . The Sefuwa's income included the *zakat* (alms), *dibalram* (road tolls), *kultingo* (tribute) and war booty. All those who participated in tax collection reserved some portion for themselves while the major title-

holders reserved large portions, paying the rest as tribute to the king. Both the *mai* and fief-holders, however, were expected to redistribute the major portions of their income as gifts to their subordinates who, in turn, were required to do the same to their followers.

The rulers of Kanem-Borno maintained their court in a style appropriate to their wealth and civilization. Even as late as the 1850s, when Kanem-Borno had passed its peak, visitors such as

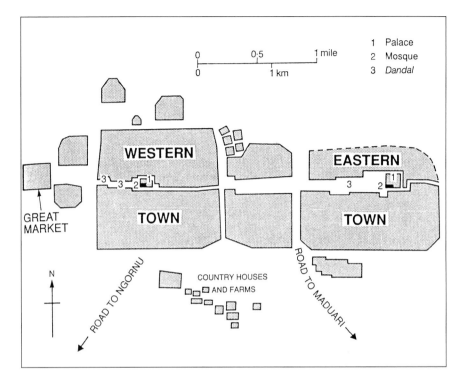

The plan of a typical Kanuri city in Kanem-Borno. The town is built in two sections, with the buildings arranged in the shape of a U. The mosque and the palace of the local leader are located at the curve of the U in each section.

45

This embroidered blouse was typical of the goods to be found in the markets of 19th-century Kanem-Borno. The local craftspeople also excelled in the creation of baskets and leather goods.

46

Gustav Nachtigal still found the royal procession an impressive sight: "In the immediate neighborhood of the prince richly clad dignitaries had assembled, wearing cloth burnuses of various colors, embroidered with gold, wide gold- or silk-embroidered trousers, and red tarbushes [brimless felt hats], with or without a turban, their faces veiled or uncovered, and riding magnificent horses with Arab saddles and stirrups. . . . Under the upper part of the left leg of each rider, there was usually a long straight sword fastened to the side of the saddle, and on the other side, on the high pommel of the saddle, hung a decorated broad-muzzled carbine [rifle]."

Kanuri cities were built in a distinctive U-shaped design: the center of the city was taken up by a wide street known as the *dendal,* and at the closed end of the dendal lay the palace of the local ruler and the mosque. Visiting Kukawa, the capital of Borno during the late 19th century, Heinrich Barth found the dendal a scene of constant activity: "This road, during the whole day, is crowded by numbers of people on horseback and on foot; free men and slaves, foreigners as well as natives, every one in his best attire, to pay his respects to the sheikh or his vizier, to deliver an errand, or to sue for justice or employment, or a present."

The market, an all-important feature of West African communities, was always located on the outskirts of the town. There, the traders from North Africa and Egypt would make their transactions, and the local people would purchase their necessities, often using strips of cotton cloth as currency. Visitors were impressed by the abundance of goods in the market, a direct result of the country's prosperity and the industrious character of its people. "Bornu, taken as a whole," wrote Nachtigal, "is in the favorable season of the year a country of great beauty, and in richness of products of the soil, in abundance of animal life, it surpasses its neighboring countries to the east. The industry of the people has converted a great part of the country into grain fields . . . and gardens, which are enlivened in the most charming way by herds of domesticated animals bursting with vigor. . . . There is . . . in the interior of Africa scarcely one country where man's activity, matching the rich capacities of the soil, has unfolded a more pleasant picture of prosperous development." Nachtigal credited much of this development to the country's "peaceful, innocent, industrious population," whose character resulted from the "blessings which came to them early of a higher civilization and orderly state development."

Much of the stability Nachtigal admired was due to the long reign of the Sefuwa and their ability to control their vast territory. However, by the time of his visit the Sefuwa's power had already crumbled, and before long Kanem-Borno itself was to lose its independence.

47

Chapter 6 | REVOLUTION AND RENEWAL

Visiting Europeans are received by a Muslim sheik and his leading officials in 19th-century Kanem-Borno. The sheik appears in the background, separated from his subjects by a ceremonial cage known as a fanadir.

Since being forced by the Bulala to relocate their capital during the 14th century, the Sefuwa had not faced a similar crisis for hundreds of years. When a new and potentially disastrous challenge arose during the 19th century, it came not from the non-Islamized peoples of the South but from the Sefuwa's fellow Muslims.

Almost since its origin, the religion of Islam had given rise to competing sects. Perhaps because of the rigorous teachings of the Koran and the close alliance of government and religion, groups of Muslims in all nations frequently believed that their rulers were straying from the path of true worship. In many of these cases reform movements arose to purify the faith. The reformers often resorted to force of arms as well as argument; as a result, a regime accused of being lax in religious matters might be overthrown and replaced by one that proposed to adhere more closely to the will of Allah. During the 19th century, such a movement was spearheaded by the Fulani people who lived to the west of Kanem-Borno.

The Fulani were wandering herders who had originally lived on the edges of the Sahara and had been among the first West Africans to adopt Islam. Formidable warriors who drew added strength from their ability to survive under harsh conditions, they gradually made their presence felt throughout the Sudan. The Fulani adhered to a strict form of worship. They had little tolerance for the luxury of royal courts or the mixing of Islamic beliefs with the practices of traditional religions. They found many followers among the lower ranks of society, such as poor peasants and slaves, who had no particular reason to admire the established order of things.

Led by Usuman dan Fodio and his son Muhammad Bello, the Fulani reform movement swept the Hausa states during the opening years of the 19th century. Wherever the reform movement was victorious, it replaced the old-style kings with Muslim rulers known as emirs or sheiks. The emirs were said to rely on Allah alone for their power and to govern solely through Islamic law; for this reason they discarded many of the royal privileges and rituals that had been common throughout the Sudan. Following this pattern, the former Hausa states gave way to a unified Muslim government, the Sokoto Caliphate. As the caliphate gained strength, the Sefuwa became the next target for the Muslim jihad, or holy war.

In 1808, the Sokoto forces, in concert with Fulani groups living in Borno, sacked Birni Gazargamu and forced Mai Ahmad, the Sefuwa king, to flee to Kanem. Realizing that his situation was desperate, Ahmad turned for help to an eminent Muslim named Muhammad al-Kanemi. Al-Kanemi was a man of mixed parentage: his mother was an Arab and his father a Kanembu, one of the black African peoples living to the west of Lake Chad. Al-Kanemi thought of himself principally as a scholar and religious leader rather than as a politician or soldier. But he responded to Ahmad's appeal and agreed to help stave off the Fulani threat.

Al-Kanemi at first tried diplomacy. He wrote to the leaders of the Sokoto Caliphate and asked why they were attacking fellow Muslims. When his reasoning failed to bring peace, he confronted the Fulani on the battlefield and drove them out of Borno. Mai Ahmad rewarded al-Kanemi with an important fiefdom centered in Ngurno. From that base al-Kanemi expanded his power, relying on a council of six close friends and a personal force of mounted Kanembu spearmen. He became so powerful that by 1820, Borno was divided into two sections, one still under Ahmad's rule, and one controlled by al-Kanemi and his supporters.

This system began to break down after the death of al-Kanemi in 1837, at which point his son Umar began to encroach on the power of the king. In 1846, the Sefuwa mai Ibrahim responded by inciting the sultan of Wadai, a neighboring state, to attack Umar. However, Umar

50

51

An engraving of
one of the Kanembu
spearmen who
made up the personal
bodyguard of Sheikh
al-Kanemi. After
defending Borno from
invading Fulani forces,
al-Kanemi became
as powerful as the
Sefuwa kings; he
maintained his own
armed forces
and occupied a
separate capital.

was victorious in battle; he took his revenge by executing Ibrahim and assuming complete control over Borno. Thus the hereditary kingship of Kanem-Borno, which had extended for 1,000 years under the Zaghawa and Sefuwa, came to an end. With the exception of Japan, no country has known a longer period of rule by a single family than the 800 years of the Sefuwa dynasty.

After a period of civil unrest during which he was briefly deposed before regaining power, Sheik Umar ruled without interruption from 1854 to his death in 1881. Under his rule, Borno enjoyed a level of prosperity not seen since the 17th century. Europeans who visited Kukawa found Umar no less impressive than his nation. Heinrich Barth described him in the following terms: "He has regular and agreeable features. . . . He is remarkably black—a real glossy black, such as is rarely seen in Bórnu, and which he has inherited undoubtedly from his mother, a Bagirmaye princess. He was very simply dressed in a light tobe, having a bernús negligently wrapped around his shoulder; round his head a dark red shawl was twisted with great care; and his face was quite uncovered, which surprised me not a little, as his father used to cover it in the Tawárek [Tuareg] fashion. He was

reclining upon a divan covered with a carpet, at the back of a fine, airy hall neatly polished." Barth generally visited the sheik early in the morning or late at night, when he was attended only by his chief official, the vizier: "But sometimes they wished me also to visit and sit with them, when they were accessible to all the people; and on these occasions the vizier took pride and delight in conversing with me about matters of science, such as the motion of the earth, or the planetary system, or subjects of that kind."

This civilized regime survived the death of Umar, but it came to an end in 1893, when Kukawa was sacked by the forces of Rabeh, an Arab soldier of fortune who invaded the central Sudan at the head of an army that had once belonged to a Middle Eastern slave trader. Rabeh attempted to establish his own kingship, but he was too late. In 1870, the European powers had decided to carve up Africa into colonies, and French troops were active throughout the Sudan. West Africans resisted valiantly, but ultimately they could not withstand the European forces with their cannons and machine guns. In 1900, the French surrounded Rabeh and killed him in battle.

In 1902, the French ceded control of Borno to the British. More inclined to rely

52

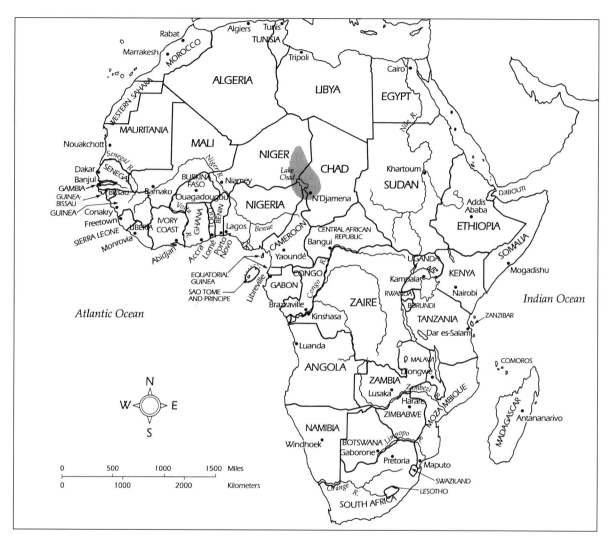

A map of contemporary Africa, with the shaded area indicating the former territory of Kanem-Borno. Kanem is now part of the Chad republic, while Borno forms an independent Muslim state in the Federal Republic of Nigeria.

53

on diplomacy than on force, the British decided that they could best rule their African colonies indirectly through tradi- tional local leaders. For this reason, the British appointed one of al-Kanemi's de- scendants sheik (*shehu* in the Kanuri

54

A 20th-century horseman attached to the retinue of the shehu of Borno. Though the centuries-long reign of the Sefuwa dynasty is now over, the glory of Kanem-Borno survives in many ancient traditions and ceremonies.

language) of Borno. In 1905, they set up a new capital, Maiduguri, in southern Borno, which was to serve both as the center of the sheikdom and of the political administration. Though the colonial government exercised ultimate control over the affairs of Borno, the British promised that they would not interfere with the practice of Islam in Borno or the 11 other Muslim states (emirates) of the North. Throughout the rest of Nigeria, as the new British colony was named, missionaries were energetically trying to convert Africans to Christianity.

Since Nigeria achieved its independence in 1960, it has emerged as the most populous (more than 110 million people in the 1990s) and prosperous of the West African nations. Borno is the second largest of Nigeria's 19 provinces, covering a territory of 46,000 square miles. Islam still reigns in the former domains of the Sefuwa kings, under the supervision of the shehu of Borno, who has inherited the title *amir al-mu'minin* (commander of the faithful). Maiduguri, a city of 250,000 inhabitants, remains the capital of the emirate.

Kanem itself now lies within the borders of the modern nation of Chad, and other parts of the former Sefuwa empire are located in the Niger Republic. But the great traditions of the Kanem-Borno empire remain in northern Nigeria with the Kanuri people. About 80 percent of the Kanuri still make their living from the land, cultivating millet as their principal crop. The Kanuri cherish their heritage, carrying out annual ceremonies at the tombs of the Sefuwa kings. Like the fearsome mounted cavalry of bygone days, Kanuri men still prize their horses and often ride in ceremonial formations to pay homage to their local leaders. Kanuri women are still identifiable by their unique hairstyle, and the Kanuri continue to build their communities in the distinctive U shape, with the house of the community's leader at the bottom of the U, facing west.

The Kanuri's faithfulness to their ancestral ways does not stem from a desire to live in the past. It is, above all, an expression of self-confidence. In the case of the Kanuri, this self-confidence derives from a deep attachment to the land and from a long tradition of successful self-government that is matched by few peoples in the world. The fortitude and courage that allow a people to endure through the centuries in a world of upheaval are summed up in a traditional Kanuri proverb: "At the bottom of patience there is heaven."

CHRONOLOGY

4th century A.D.   Camels are introduced into Africa; trade increases between North Africa and the Sudan; Sao people flourish in the Lake Chad region

7th century   Muslims conquer Arabia, Egypt, North Africa, and Spain

9th century   Zaghawa establish themselves as rulers in Kanem, north of Lake Chad

11th century   Kanem begins expansion in central Sudan under the Zaghawa kings and extends its territory into the Sahara

1067   Hawwa (Hu) becomes the first Muslim ruler of Kanem

1075   Hummay, the first ruler of the Sefuwa dynasty, becomes king of Kanem

1210–48   Reign of Dunama Dibalami; Sefuwa take control of Borno, establishing the dual kingdom of Kanem-Borno; Sefuwa control entire trade route between Fezzan and Lake Chad

14th century   Kanem-Borno disrupted by civil wars between rivals for the throne; Bulala wage war on Kanem, killing four Sefuwa kings within seven years; Mai Umar ibn Idris moves his capital to Borno

1465–97   Reign of Ali Ghaji, who builds a new capital at Birni Gazargamu and restores stability to kingdom of Kanem-Borno

1564–96	Reign of Idris Alooma, who subdues the Bulala, introduces innovations in warfare, technology, and government, and forges alliances with Morocco and the Ottoman Empire
17th century	Kanem-Borno enjoys its golden age; Kanuri people emerge as the kingdom's dominant ethnic group
1808–20	Muslim reformers conquer Hausaland and then attack Borno; Muhammad al-Kanemi drives out the invaders and expands his sheikdom until it rivals the regime of the Sefuwa kings
1846	End of the Sefuwa dynasty and of the 1,000-year tradition of kingship in Kanem-Borno
1854–81	Reign of Sheik Umar; Borno enjoys high level of prosperity and culture
1902	British take control of Borno but maintain the emirate under the descendants of al-Kanemi
1960	Former British colony of Nigeria gains its independence; Borno becomes one of 19 provinces in the Federal Republic of Nigeria; Kanem is incorporated into the Chad Republic

57

FURTHER READING

Ajayi, J. F. Ade, and Michael Crowder, eds. *History of West Africa.* 2 vols. New York: Columbia University Press, 1973.

Barth, Henry. *Travels and Discoveries in North and Central Africa in the Years 1849–1855.* 3 vols. New York: Harper & Brothers, 1857.

Cohen, Ronald. *The Kanuri of Borno.* New York: Holt, Rinehart & Winston, 1967.

Connah, Graham. *African Civilizations.* Cambridge: Cambridge University Press, 1987.

Davidson, Basil. *Africa in History.* Rev. ed. New York: Collier, 1991.

———. *The African Genius.* Boston: Little, Brown, 1969.

———. *The Lost Cities of Africa.* Rev. ed. Boston: Little, Brown, 1987.

Davidson, Basil, with F. K. Buah and the advice of J. F. A. Ajayi. *A History of West Africa, 1000–1800.* New rev. ed. London: Longman, 1977.

Gillon, Werner. *A Short History of African Art.* New York: Penguin, 1986.

Grove, A. T. *The Changing Geography of Africa.* 2nd ed. London: Oxford University Press, 1993.

Hull, Richard W. *African Cities and Towns Before the European Conquest.* New York: Norton, 1976.

Ikimi, Obaro, ed. *Groundwork of Nigerian History.* London: Heinemann, 1980.

Koslow, Philip. *Centuries of Greatness: The West African Kingdoms, 750–1900.* New York: Chelsea House, 1994.

Kwamena-Poh, Michael, et al. *African History in Maps.* London: Longman, 1982.

Lange, Dierk. *A Sudanic Chronicle: The Borno Expeditions of Idris Alauma.* Stuttgart: Steiner Verlag, 1987.

Nachtigal, Gustav. *Sahara and Sudan.* Translated by Allan G. B. Fisher and Humphrey J. Fisher. 4 vols. London: Hurst, 1971–87.

Palmer, H. R. *Sudanese Memoirs.* London: Cass, 1967.

Park, Mungo. *Travels in the Interior Districts of Africa.* 1799. Reprint. New York: Arno Press / New York Times, 1971.

Parrinder, Geoffrey. *Religion in Africa.* New York: Praeger, 1969.

Trimingham, John S. *A History of Islam in West Africa.* London: University of Oxford Press, 1962.

———. *Islam in West Africa.* Oxford: Clarendon Press, 1959.

UNESCO General History of Africa. 7 vols. Berkeley: University of California Press, 1981–92.

Webster, J. B., and A. A. Boahen, with M. Tidy. *The Revolutionary Years: West Africa Since 1800.* New ed. London: Longman, 1980.

GLOSSARY

archaeology   the study of the physical remains of past human societies

Borno   the state governed by the Sefuwa kings after the mid-13th century; now an emirate in the Republic of Nigeria

dendal   the main thoroughfare of a traditional U-shaped Kanuri town

emirate   a state in Asia, Africa, or the Middle East governed by an independent Muslim chief

feudalism   a political system based on the mutual obligations of lords and vassals

fief   an area controlled by a vassal under grant from a feudal lord

Islam   the religion based upon worship of Allah and acceptance of Muhammad as his prophet

Kanem   the original kingdom of the Sefuwa; now part of the Chad Republic

Kanuri   the dominant ethnic group of Kanem-Borno, which emerged from the intermarriage of Nilo-Saharan–speaking groups from Kanem with Chadic-speaking groups living south of Lake Chad

Koran   the holy book of Islam

mai	title used by the kings of Kanem-Borno
millet	a variety of grasses cultivated for their edible seeds; the principal crop grown by the Kanuri of Borno
mosque	a Muslim house of worship
Muslim	one who follows the religion of Islam
Sefuwa	ruling dynasty of Kanem-Bornu from the 11th through the 19th centuries
sheik	a Muslim chief; *shehu* in the Kanuri language
Sudan	the region of sub-Saharan Africa stretching from the Atlantic coast to the valley of the Nile River; derives from *Bilad al-Sudan*, Arabic for "land of the black peoples"
tobe	a loose cotton garment traditionally worn by the Kanuri
vassal	an individual under the protection of a feudal lord, enjoying social and political benefits in return for pledges of loyalty and service
vizier	a high officer in a Muslim state
Zaghawa	Saharan people who became the first rulers of Kanem during the 9th century

INDEX

PHILIP KOSLOW earned his B.A. and M.A. degrees from New York University and went on to teach and conduct research at Oxford University, where his interest in medieval European and African history was awakened. The editor of numerous volumes for young adults, he is also the author of *El Cid* in the Chelsea House HISPANICS OF ACHIEVEMENT series and of *Centuries of Greatness: The West African Kingdoms, 750–1900* in Chelsea House's MILESTONES IN BLACK AMERICAN HISTORY series.

PICTURE CREDITS

966.9   Koslow, Philip.
KOS
         Kanem-Borno.

$15.95   11253